Presented to

Jacob Warren

by
Zion Lutheran Church
Anoka, MN

Confirmation Ministry
2003-2004

LUTHER'S SMALL CATECHISM

Published by
Augsburg Fortress
Minneapolis

A Contemporary Translation of
LUTHER'S SMALL CATECHISM

Original copyright © 1994 Augsburg Fortress, Publishers
Introduction and translation by Timothy J. Wengert

Jeffrey S. Nelson and Elizabeth Drotning, editors
Nick Markell, Markell Studios, liturgical artist

Scripture quotations are from New Revised Standard Version Bible,
copyright © 1989 Division of Christian Education of the National
Council of the Churches of Christ in the United States of America.
Used by permission.

The following is reprinted from *Lutheran Book of Worship*, copyright ©
1978: Individual Confession and Forgiveness; Holy Communion words
of institution; the Marriage service; the service of Holy Baptism.

The English translations of the Lord's Prayer and the Apostles' Creed
are prepared by the International Consultation on English Texts [ICET],
copyright © 1970, 1971, and 1975.

Quotations from *Luther's Works* Vol. 50 copyright © 1975 Fortress
Press and Vol. 51 copyright © 1959 Fortress Press.

The paper used in this publication meets the minimum requirements of
American National Standard for Information Sciences—Permanence of
Paper for Printed Materials, ANSI Z329.48-1984.

Manufactured in the U.S.A.   ISBN 0-8006-4282-3

10 09 08 07 06 05 04 03 02 01   1 2 3 4 5 6 7 8 9 10

ISBN 0-8066-4282-3
90000
9 780806 642826

CONTENTS

INTRODUCTION

This introduction to the Small Catechism has three parts: "Where Do Catechisms Come From?," "What Martin Luther Added to the Catechism," and "Ways to Use this Book."

Where Do Catechisms Come From?

In 1529 Martin Luther, a pastor in the German town of Wittenberg and teacher at the university there, published his explanations to the chief parts of the Christian faith. These explanations were first produced on individual sheets and sold for a few pennies each. By the middle of 1529 printers in Wittenberg and elsewhere had collected them into what they called an *enchiridion* or handbook. Luther added a preface, which told pastors how to use the book, and he also attached several other sections to the end of it. By the end of the year printers had given this handbook a subtitle by which we know it today, *The Small Catechism of Martin Luther*. They gave it this name because in the same year Luther published a set of his sermons on the same topics. This book of sermons, then called *The German Catechism*, is now known as the Large Catechism.

But the term *catechism* is much older than Luther's work from 1529. It comes from the Greek *kata-echo*, which means "to repeat back." Already by the year A.D. 400, Latin-speaking Christians used the word *catechism* to describe the basic instruction given to new Christians. As they learned, they recited the things they heard from their teachers. By the Middle Ages *catechism* had come to mean the three things that all Christians should know: the Ten Commandments, the Apostles' Creed, and the Lord's Prayer. By the time Martin Luther was growing up in central Europe during the 1490s, pastors were required to teach these three things to all adults and children and to preach on them during weekday services four times a year. When Luther became an assistant preacher in 1514, he preached on these three chief parts. Some of his sermons were copied down and published. In 1528, during the absence of Wittenberg's head pastor, John Bugenhagen, Luther preached again on the three chief parts. The Small and Large Catechisms came from these sermons.

What Martin Luther Added to the Catechism

As Martin Luther was teaching these three chief parts to children and adults in Wittenberg, he added some things that his own congregation probably thought of as very new. In fact these new parts go back to the very beginning of Christianity and the good news of Jesus' death and resurrection. Combined with the original catechism, these additions have helped people from Luther's day right down to our own times hear and understand the heart of the Christian faith. Learning what Luther added to the three chief parts of the early catechism may help you use this book well.

1. Two "New" Chief Parts

As the table of contents shows, to the original three chief parts of the catechism Martin Luther added two more: explanations of Holy Baptism and Holy Communion. We often call them sacraments, or visible Words of God, because they combine physical elements with God's command and promise. Here God comes to us in very personal ways: combining God's name and ours in Baptism and feeding our bodies with Christ's body and blood in the Lord's Supper. By including these sacraments—the visible Words—with God's spoken Word in the Ten Commandments, Apostles' Creed, and Lord's Prayer, Martin Luther reminds us that Christianity is not just about memorizing rules or doctrines or prayers, but that it focuses on what God does for us in Jesus Christ.

When Christians were asked in Luther's day to define the church, they responded that the church is not so much a building or an organization but an event that the Holy Spirit brings into being wherever the Word of God is preached and the sacraments are administered to call and gather believers. By including the sacraments in the Small Catechism, Luther defines *church* for everyone who uses this book. Here God is at work making us believers.

2. *The "New" Order*

Many of the popular catechetical booklets published before Luther's Small Catechism emphasized what we must do to avoid God's anger and earn God's favor. Many times we may also think that God and Christianity are only about rules and regulations. The order of the Small Catechism helps correct that misunderstanding and focuses our attention on God's gifts to us. Luther insisted that Christians begin with the Ten Commandments, which show us God's demands and our inability to fulfill them, and then move to the Apostles' Creed, which declares what God does for us, and then to the Lord's Prayer, which teaches us where we may go for help.

The sacraments, too, give us what we need most from God: forgiveness of sins, life, and salvation. Thus, mirroring Baptism, the Small Catechism moves from the "drowning" of the old person and our sins to the raising up of the new in faith.

One time Martin Luther reflected on this order and said that it was like a physician who begins with the diagnosis (the Ten Commandments) before offering treatment (the good news in the Apostles' Creed and Lord's Prayer). The point of the Small Catechism is to give us comfort and support when we face problems in our Christian life. At least that is what Katherine Luther, Martin Luther's wife, once said. In a letter to her near the end of his life, Martin Luther tried to calm her worries about his health by reminding her, "You, dear Katie, read [my sermons on the Gospel of] John and the Small Catechism, about which you once said: 'Everything in this book has been said about me.' For you prefer to worry about me instead of letting God worry" (*Luther's Works*, 50:302).

3. *The Question*

Other pastors in Martin Luther's day wrote catechisms with many complicated questions and answers. Luther's Small Catechism sticks for the most part to one simple question: "What is this?" (Other translations of the Small Catechism often expand this basic question to "What does this mean?") In fact, Luther is not so much interested in the deeper, hidden meanings of these chief parts as in basic definitions, such as "What is the First Commandment? or Amen? or Baptism?"

Luther used this simple question because he had found it effective when teaching Wittenberg's young people the catechism in his sermons. In 1529 he also had another inspiration for using such a simple question. Although he was forty-five years old, he had been a father for only three years. At that time little Hans Luther was running around the house pointing at everything and asking his father, "*Was ist das?*" ("What is this?"). His father used Hans' question in the Small Catechism.

4. *Luther's Faith*

This brings us to another important contribution in Martin Luther's little book. Most of the time when we learn the Small Catechism, the teacher asks the question and the student gives the answer. But when Luther was writing this material, he also was answering the questions many Christians were asking him: "What is this? How does this happen?" Thus, the Small Catechism is Martin Luther's confession of faith in God. In it, Luther tells us what these things are for him and for us. You may discover that not only is Luther asking, "What is this?" but God also is asking. As you study the Small Catechism, you, too, are invited to confess, "God has created me; Jesus is my Lord; the Holy Spirit calls me and gathers me into the church."

5. *The Center*

The center of Martin Luther's confession of faith in the Small Catechism is the Apostles' Creed—that is, faith in God's promises. And the center of the Creed is God our creator, who, in the death and resurrection of Jesus Christ, rescues us from all evil. By the Holy Spirit God creates and strengthens our faith in Christ and his forgiveness. God's commandments, grounded in the First Commandment, show how much we need faith to "fear, love, and trust God." The Lord's Prayer is anchored by our heavenly Father's promise to listen and to act. The sacraments proclaim forgiveness and rescue in Jesus Christ.

Ways to Use this Book

Before Martin Luther's death in 1546 and certainly after that time, the Small Catechism became more and more simply a textbook for young students to memorize and recite. Some parts were omitted, others tacked on. Whole books were written explaining Luther's explanations!

The Small Catechism presented here follows Luther's original concept more closely and allows us to use this book both in and outside the classroom. Here are some suggestions for use.

1. Handbook for the Household

When each individual part of the Small Catechism was sold separately, each sheet had this heading: "...in a simple way in which the head of a house is to present them to the household." In a sermon delivered in November 1528, Luther addresses the fathers and mothers by saying, "Every father of a family is a bishop in his house and the wife a bishopess. Therefore remember that you in your homes are to help us carry on the ministry as we do in the church. If we do this we shall have a gracious God, who will defend us from all evil and in all evil" (*Luther's Works*, 51:137). Luther wrote the Small Catechism for the home, so that parents could explain to their children in simple terms the most important things in the Christian faith. For Luther the household is a house church.

Several additions to the Small Catechism underscore Luther's concern. There are sections for morning and evening prayers and for prayers before and after mealtimes. There is an entire section entitled "A Chart of Some Bible Passages for the Household" (formerly called "Table of Duties"), in which Luther uses Bible verses to describe how we are to behave toward one another as parents, children, married people, workers, and the like. Also included in all booklet versions of the Small Catechism during Luther's lifetime and beyond were the services of Marriage and Holy Baptism: Marriage because most households in Luther's day came into being at the time of marriage; Baptism because that begins the life of faith for all Christians.

We can continue to use these things in our homes today. You can add Luther's table prayers to the ones your family may already be using. If you are not accustomed to praying in the morning or evening, Luther's brief prayers can strengthen your faith. The Bible passages Luther collected are only a few of the many that describe how Christ frees a Christian in faith toward God and love for one another. In this edition we have kept Luther's own prefaces to the Marriage and Baptism services but replaced the orders of worship with material from today's *Lutheran Book of Worship*.

2. Prayer Book

One of the first ways Martin Luther taught people about the catechism was through prayer. Luther included suggestions for prayers in the morning and evening and at meals. Many of these prayers are from prayers written before Luther's time.

There are three ways to use the Small Catechism for prayer. First, you can use the prayers he suggests in your own personal or family devotions. Second, you can use the explanations of the Lord's Prayer to help you understand what we ask God for in that prayer. Third, you can actually use the various parts of the Small Catechism as the basis for your own prayers. Martin Luther described how he himself prayed the Ten Commandments, Apostles' Creed, and Lord's Prayer in a published letter written to his barber, Master Peter, who had asked him how to pray. Each commandment, article of the Creed, or petition of the Lord's Prayer suggests things we can request from God or thank God for receiving.

3. Worship Book

Along with the prayers, many early editions of the Small Catechism also included parts of the worship service to encourage worship in the household and the congregation. We have included the Services of Baptism, Marriage, and Individual Confession and Forgiveness. The five chief parts of the Small Catechism also have their place in worship. The Ten Commandments and Confession prepare us for Confession and Forgiveness. The Apostles' Creed and Lord's Prayer are used in many worship services. Holy Baptism and Holy Communion are two of the things that create the Christian church and gather it in worship around God's forgiveness in Jesus Christ.

The various parts of the Small Catechism also help us listen to the lessons and the sermon, since almost all of them will relate to one section of the catechism or another. The better we know the Small Catechism, the easier it will be to understand and hear God's Word in the readings and preaching. As you listen, ask yourself, "What part of the catechism is this?"

May this little book open up the Bible to you and strengthen your faith!

Timothy J. Wengert
Philadelphia, Pennsylvania

Note to the reader:
There are other translations of the Small Catechism your congregation may also be using. This translation is based primarily on the edition of Luther's Small Catechism published at Wittenberg in 1536, in consultation with other authorial editions. It is part of a larger translation that appears in an edition of The Book of Concord (Minneapolis: Fortress Press, 2000). That edition includes many more historical notes for pastors and teachers.

LUTHER'S PREFACE TO THE
SMALL CATECHISM OF 1529*

Martin Luther, to all faithful and upright pastors and preachers:

Grace, mercy, and peace in Jesus Christ our Lord.

The deplorable, wretched shortcomings that I recently encountered while I was a visitor has constrained and compelled me to prepare this catechism, or Christian instruction, in such a brief, plain, and simple version. Dear God, what misery I beheld! The ordinary person, especially in the villages, knows absolutely nothing about the Christian faith, and unfortunately many pastors are completely unskilled and incompetent teachers. Yet they are all supposed to bear the name Christian, to be baptized, and to receive the Holy Sacrament, even though they do not know the Lord's Prayer, the Creed, or the Ten Commandments! As a result they live like simple cattle or irrational pigs and, despite the fact that the gospel has returned, have mastered the fine art of misusing all their freedom.

---

* Here Luther advises pastors on how to teach Christian doctrine and use this book.

O you bishops! How are you going to answer to Christ, now that you have so shamefully allowed the people to wander off and have not exercised your office for even a single second? May you escape punishment for this! You forbid the cup to the laity in the Lord's Supper* and insist on observance of your human laws, while never even bothering to ask whether the people know the Lord's Prayer, the Creed, the Ten Commandments, or a single section of God's Word. Shame on you forever!

Therefore, my dear sirs and brothers, who are either pastors or preachers, I beg all of you for God's sake to take up your office boldly, to have pity on your people, who are entrusted to you, and to help us bring the catechism to the people, especially to the young. Moreover, I ask that those unable to do any better take up these charts and versions and read them to the people word for word in the following manner:

In the first place, the preacher should above all take care to avoid changes or variations in the text and version of the Ten Commandments, the Lord's Prayer, the Creed, the sacraments, but instead adopt a single version, stick with it, and always use the same one year after year. For the young and the unlettered people must be taught with a single, fixed text and version. Otherwise, if someone teaches one way now and another way next year—even for the sake of making improvements—the people become quite easily confused, and all the time and effort will go for naught.

The dear church fathers also understood this well. They used one form for the Lord's Prayer, the Creed, and the Ten Commandments. Therefore, we, too, should teach these parts to the young and to people who cannot read in such a way that we neither change a single

* In Luther's day only priests received the wine in the Lord's Supper.

syllable nor present or recite it differently from one year to the next. Therefore, choose for yourself whatever version you want and stick with it for good. To be sure, when you preach to educated and intelligent people, then you may demonstrate your erudition and discuss these parts with as much complexity and from as many different angles as you can. But with the young people, stick with a fixed, unchanging version and form. To begin with, teach them these parts: the Ten Commandments, the Creed, the Lord's Prayer, etc., following the text word for word, so that they can also repeat it back to you and learn it by heart.

You should tell those who do not want to learn these things how they deny Christ, are not Christians, should also not be admitted to the Sacrament, should not be sponsors for children at Baptism, and should not exercise any aspect of Christian freedom, but instead should simply be sent back home to the pope and his officials and, along with them, to the devil himself. Moreover, you should tell them how their parents and employers ought to deny them food and drink and advise them that the prince is disposed to drive such coarse people out of the country.

Although no one can or should force another person to believe, nevertheless one should insist upon and hold the masses to this: that they know what is right and wrong according to the standards of those among whom they wish to reside, eat, and earn a living. For example, if people want to live in a particular city, they ought to know and abide by the city's laws, whose protection they enjoy, no matter whether they believe or are at heart scoundrels and villains.

In the second place, once the people have learned the text well, then teach them to understand it, too, so that they know what it means. Take up again the form offered in these charts or some other short form that you may prefer. Then adhere to it without changing a single syllable, just as was stated above regarding the text. Moreover, allow yourself ample time for it, because you need not take up all the parts at once but may instead handle them one at a time. After the people understand the First Commandment well, then take up the Second, and so on. Otherwise they will be so overwhelmed that they will hardly remember a single thing.

In the third place, after you have taught the people a short catechism like this one, then take up a longer catechism and impart to them a richer and fuller understanding. Using such a catechism, explain each individual commandment, petition, or part with its various works, benefits and blessings, harm and danger, as you find treated at length in so many booklets. In particular, put the greatest stress on that commandment or part where your people experience the greatest need. For example, you must strongly emphasize the Seventh Commandment, dealing with stealing, to artisans and shopkeepers and even to farmers and household workers, because rampant among such people are all kinds of dishonesty and thievery.

Likewise, you must emphasize the Fourth Commandment to children and the common people, so that they are orderly, faithful, obedient, and peaceful. Always adduce many examples from the Scriptures where God either punished or blessed such people. In particular, at this point also urge governing authorities and parents to rule well and to send their children to school. Point out how they are obliged to do so and what a damnable sin they commit if they do not, for thereby, as the worst enemies of God and humanity, they overthrow and lay waste both the kingdom of God and of the world. Explain very clearly what kind of horrible damage they do when they do not help to train children as pastors, preachers, civil servants, etc., and tell them that God will punish them dreadfully for this. For in our day and age it is necessary to preach about these things. The extent to which parents and governing authorities are now sinning in these matters defies description. The devil, too, intends to do something horrible in all this.

Finally, because the tyranny of the pope* has been abolished, people no longer want to receive the Sacrament [of the Altar], and they treat it with contempt. This, too, needs to be stressed, while keeping in mind that we should not compel anyone to believe or to receive the Sacrament and should not fix any law or time or place for it.** Instead, we should preach in such a way that the people make themselves come without our law and just plain compel us pastors to administer the Sacrament to them. This can be done by telling them: You have to worry that whoever does not desire or receive the Sacrament at the very least around four times a year despises the Sacrament and is no Christian, just as anyone who does not listen to or believe the gospel is no Christian. For Christ did not say, "Omit this," or "Despise this," but instead, "Do this, as often as you drink it..." He really wants it to be done and not completely omitted or despised. "*Do* this," he says.

Those who do not hold the Sacrament in high esteem indicate that they have no sin, no flesh, no devil, no world, no death, no dangers, no hell. That is, they believe they have none of these things, although they are up to their ears in them and belong to the devil twice over. On the other hand, they indicate that they need no grace, no life, no paradise, no heaven, no Christ, no God, nor any other good thing. For if they believed that

---

* Luther's strong language reflects his ongoing struggle with the institutional church of his day.
** In Luther's day all Christians had to commune between Easter and 10 days after Pentecost.

they possessed so much evil and needed so much good, they would not neglect the Sacrament, in which help against such evil is provided and in which so much good is given. It would not be necessary to compel them with any law to receive the Sacrament. Instead, they would come on their own, rushing and running to it; they would compel themselves to come and would insist that you give them the Sacrament.

For these reasons you do not need to make any law concerning this, as they did under the pope. Only emphasize clearly the benefit and the harm, the need and the blessing, the danger and the salvation regarding this Sacrament. Then they will doubtless come on their own without any compulsion. If they do not come, give up on them and tell them that those who do not pay attention to or feel their great need and God's gracious help belong to the devil. However, if you either do not urge such participation or make it into a law or poison, then it is your fault if they despise the Sacrament. How can they help but neglect it, if you sleep and remain silent?

Therefore, pastors and preachers, take note! Our office has now become a completely different one than it was under the pope. It has now become serious and salutary. Thus, it now involves much toil and work, danger and temptation, and in addition little reward or gratitude in the world. But Christ himself will be our reward, so long as we labor faithfully. May the Father of all grace grant it, to whom be praise and thanks in eternity through Christ, our Lord. Amen.

THE TEN COMMANDMENTS

You shall have no other gods.
> I, the Lord your God, am a jealous God,
> punishing children for the iniquity of parents
> to the third and the fourth generation of those
> who reject me, but showing steadfast love
> to the thousandth generation of those who
> love me and keep my commandments.

You shall not make wrongful use
> of the name of the Lord your God.

Remember the sabbath day, and keep it holy.

Honor your father and your mother.

You shall not murder.

You shall not commit adultery.

You shall not steal.

You shall not bear false witness against your
> neighbor.

You shall not covet your neighbor's house.

You shall not covet your neighbor's wife,
> or male or female slave, or ox, or donkey,
> or anything that belongs to your neighbor.

from Exodus 20:1-17

THE FIRST COMMANDMENT

You shall have no other gods.

What is this?

Answer: We are to fear, love, and trust God above all things.

THE SECOND COMMANDMENT

You shall not make wrongful use of the name of the Lord your God.

What is this?

Answer: We are to fear and love God, so that we do not curse, swear, practice magic, lie, or deceive using God's name, but instead use that very name in every time of need to call on, pray to, praise, and give thanks to God.

THE THIRD COMMANDMENT

Remember the sabbath day, and keep it holy.

What is this?

Answer: We are to fear and love God, so that we do not despise God's Word or preaching, but instead keep that Word holy and gladly hear and learn it.

THE FOURTH COMMANDMENT

Honor your father and your mother.

What is this?

Answer: We are to fear and love God, so that we neither despise nor anger our parents and others in authority, but instead honor, serve, obey, love, and respect them.

THE FIFTH COMMANDMENT

You shall not murder.

What is this?

Answer: We are to fear and love God, so that we neither endanger nor harm the lives of our neighbors, but instead help and support them in all of life's needs.

THE SIXTH COMMANDMENT

You shall not commit adultery.

What is this?

Answer: We are to fear and love God, so that we lead pure and decent lives in word and deed, and each of us loves and honors his or her spouse.

THE SEVENTH COMMANDMENT

You shall not steal.

What is this?

Answer: We are to fear and love God, so that we neither take our neighbors' money or property nor use shoddy merchandise or crooked deals to obtain it for ourselves, but instead help them to improve and protect their property and income.

THE EIGHTH COMMANDMENT

You shall not bear false witness against your neighbor.

What is this?

Answer: We are to fear and love God, so that we do not tell lies about our neighbors, betray or slander them, or destroy their reputations. Instead we are to come to their defense, speak well of them, and interpret everything they do in the best possible light.

THE NINTH COMMANDMENT

You shall not covet your neighbor's house.

What is this?

Answer: We are to fear and love God, so that we do not try to trick our neighbors out of their inheritance or property or try to get it for ourselves by claiming to have a legal right to it and the like, but instead be of help and service to them in keeping what is theirs.

THE TENTH COMMANDMENT

You shall not covet your neighbor's wife, or male or female slave, or ox, or donkey, or anything that belongs to your neighbor.

What is this?

Answer: We are to fear and love God, so that we do not entice, force, or steal away from our neighbors their spouses, workers, or livestock, but instead urge them to stay and remain loyal to our neighbors.

THE APOSTLES' CREED

I believe in God, the Father almighty,
    creator of heaven and earth.

I believe in Jesus Christ, his only Son, our Lord.
    He was conceived by the power of the Holy Spirit
        and born of the virgin Mary.
    He suffered under Pontius Pilate,
        was crucified, died, and was buried.
    He descended into hell.*
    On the third day he rose again.
    He ascended into heaven,
        and is seated at the right hand of the Father.
    He will come again to judge the living and the dead.

I believe in the Holy Spirit,
    the holy catholic Church,
    the communion of saints,
    the forgiveness of sins,
    the resurrection of the body,
    and the life everlasting. Amen.

*Or, He descended to the dead.

THE FIRST ARTICLE: ON CREATION

I believe in God, the Father almighty,
    creator of heaven and earth.

What is this?

Answer: I believe that God has created me together with all creatures. God has given me and still preserves my body and soul: eyes, ears, and all limbs and senses; reason and all mental faculties. In addition, God daily and abundantly provides shoes and clothing, food and drink, house and home, spouse and children, fields, livestock, and all property—along with all the necessities and nourishment for this body and life. God protects me against all danger and shields and preserves me from all evil. God does all this out of pure, father-ly, and divine goodness and mercy, without any merit or worthiness of mine at all! For all of this I owe it to God to thank and praise, serve and obey him. This is most certainly true.

THE SECOND ARTICLE:
ON REDEMPTION

I believe in Jesus Christ, his only Son, our Lord.
> He was conceived by the power of the Holy
> > Spirit and born of the virgin Mary.
> He suffered under Pontius Pilate,
> > was crucified, died, and was buried.
> He descended into hell.
> On the third day he rose again.
> He ascended into heaven,
> > and is seated at the right hand of the
> > Father.
> He will come again to judge the living and the
> dead.

What is this?

Answer: I believe that Jesus Christ, true God, begotten of the Father in eternity, and also true human being, born of the virgin Mary, is my Lord. He has redeemed me, a lost and condemned person. He has purchased and freed me from all sins, from death, and from the power of the devil, not with gold or silver but with his holy, precious blood and with his innocent suffering and death. He has done all this in order that I may belong to him, live under him in his kingdom, and serve him in eternal righteousness, innocence, and blessedness, just as he is risen from the dead and lives and rules in eternity. This is most certainly true.

THE THIRD ARTICLE:
ON BEING MADE HOLY

I believe in the Holy Spirit,
    the holy catholic Church,
    the communion of saints,
    the forgiveness of sins,
    the resurrection of the body,
    and the life everlasting. Amen.

What is this?

Answer: I believe that by my own understanding or strength I cannot believe in Jesus Christ my Lord or come to him, but instead the Holy Spirit has called me through the gospel, enlightened me with his gifts, made me holy, and kept me in the true faith, just as he calls, gathers, enlightens, and makes holy the whole Christian church on earth and keeps it with Jesus Christ in the one common, true faith. Daily in this Christian church the Holy Spirit abundantly forgives all sins—mine and those of all believers. On the last day the Holy Spirit will raise me and all the dead and will give to me and all believers in Christ eternal life. This is most certainly true.

THE LORD'S PRAYER

Our Father in heaven,
    hallowed be your name,
    your kingdom come,
    your will be done, on earth as in heaven.
Give us today our daily bread.
Forgive us our sins
    as we forgive those who sin against us.
Save us from the time of trial
    and deliver us from evil.
For the kingdom, the power,
    and the glory are yours,
    now and forever. Amen.

Our Father, who art in heaven,
    hallowed be thy name,
    thy kingdom come,
    thy will be done, on earth as it is in heaven.
Give us this day our daily bread;
and forgive us our trespasses,
    as we forgive those who trespass against us;
and lead us not into temptation,
    but deliver us from evil.
For thine is the kingdom,
    and the power, and the glory,
    forever and ever. Amen.

INTRODUCTION

Our Father in heaven.

What is this?

Answer: With these words God wants to attract us, so that we believe he is truly our Father and we are truly his children, in order that we may ask him boldly and with complete confidence, just as loving children ask their loving father.*

---

* Luther added this explanation to the Small Catechism in 1531 when his oldest child was five years old.

THE FIRST PETITION*

Hallowed be your name.

What is this?

Answer: It is true that God's name is holy in itself, but we ask in this prayer that it may also become holy in and among us.

How does this come about?

Answer: Whenever the Word of God is taught clearly and purely and we, as God's children, also live holy lives according to it. To this end help us, dear Father in heaven! However, whoever teaches and lives otherwise than the Word of God teaches, dishonors God's name among us. Preserve us from this, heavenly Father!

* The word *petition* means "request."

THE SECOND PETITION

Your kingdom come.

What is this?

Answer: In fact, God's kingdom comes on its own without our prayer, but we ask in this prayer that it may also come to us.

How does this come about?

Answer: Whenever our heavenly Father gives us his Holy Spirit, so that through the Holy Spirit's grace we believe God's Holy Word and live godly lives here in time and hereafter in eternity.

THE THIRD PETITION

Your will be done, on earth as in heaven.

What is this?

Answer: In fact, God's good and gracious will comes about without our prayer, but we ask in this prayer that it may also come about in and among us.

How does this come about?

Answer: Whenever God breaks and hinders every evil scheme and will of the devil, the world, and our flesh that would not allow us to hallow God's name and would prevent the coming of his kingdom. And God's will is done whenever God strengthens us and keeps us steadfast in his Word and in faith until the end of our lives. This is God's gracious and good will.

THE FOURTH PETITION

Give us today our daily bread.

What is this?

Answer: In fact, God gives daily bread without our prayer, even to all evil people, but we ask in this prayer that God cause us to recognize what our daily bread is and to receive it with thanksgiving.

What then does "daily bread" mean?

Answer: Everything our bodies need such as food, drink, clothing, shoes, house, home, fields, livestock, money, property, an upright spouse, upright children, upright members of the household, upright and faithful rulers, good government, good weather, peace, health, decency, honor, good friends, faithful neighbors, and the like.

THE FIFTH PETITION

Forgive us our sins
    as we forgive those
        who sin against us.

What is this?

Answer: We ask in this prayer that our heavenly Father would not regard our sins or deny these petitions on their account, for we are worthy of nothing for which we ask, nor have we earned it. Instead we ask that God would give us all things by grace, for we sin daily and indeed earn only punishment. So, on the other hand, we, too, truly want to forgive heartily and do good gladly to those who sin against us.

THE SIXTH PETITION

Save us from the time of trial.*

What is this?

Answer: It is true that God tempts no one, but we ask in this prayer that God would preserve and keep us, so that the devil, the world, and our flesh may not deceive us or mislead us into false belief, despair, and other great and shameful sins, and that, although we may be attacked by them, we may finally prevail and gain the victory.

*The version of the Lord's Prayer used by Luther employed the word *temptation* in place of "the time of trial."

THE SEVENTH PETITION

And deliver us from evil.

What is this?

Answer: We ask in this prayer, as in a summary,
that our Father in heaven may deliver us from all
kinds of evil—affecting body or soul, property or
reputation—and at last, when our final hour comes,
may grant us a blessed end and take us by grace
from this valley of tears to himself in heaven.

CONCLUSION*

For the kingdom, the power,
    and the glory are yours,
    now and forever.

What is this?

Answer: That I should be certain that such petitions
are acceptable to and heard by our Father in heaven, for God himself commanded us to pray like this
and has promised to hear us.

Amen.

What is this?

Answer: "Amen, amen" means "Yes, yes, it is going
to come about just like this."

* Some later editions of the catechism, printed after Luther's death, add this conclusion, commonly called the Doxology. Although found in Erasmus's editions of the Greek New Testament and in Luther's translation of that into German, Luther himself consistently followed the medieval practice and omitted it.

THE SACRAMENT OF
HOLY BAPTISM

1. What is Baptism?

Answer: Baptism is not simply plain water. Instead it is water used according to God's command and connected with God's Word.

What then is this Word of God?

Answer: Where our Lord Jesus Christ says in Matthew 28:19, "Go therefore and make disciples of all nations, baptizing them in the name of the Father and of the Son and of the Holy Spirit."

2. What gifts or benefits does Baptism grant?

Answer: It brings about forgiveness of sins, redeems from death and the devil, and gives eternal salvation to all who believe it, as the Word and promise of God declare.

What is this Word and promise of God?

Answer: Where our Lord Jesus Christ says in Mark 16:16, "The one who believes and is baptized will be saved; but the one who does not believe will be condemned."

3. *How can water do such great things?*

Answer: Clearly the water does not do it, but the Word of God, which is with, in, and among the water, and faith, which trusts this Word of God in the water. For without the Word of God the water is plain water and not a baptism, but with the Word of God it is a baptism, that is, a grace-filled water of life and a "bath of the new birth in the Holy Spirit." As St. Paul says to Titus in 3:5-8, "He saved us, not because of any works of righteousness that we had done, but according to his mercy, through the water of rebirth and renewal by the Holy Spirit. This Spirit he poured out on us richly through Jesus Christ our Savior, so that, having been justified by his grace, we might become heirs according to the hope of eternal life. The saying is sure."*

* In Luther's translation of Titus, the last line reads, "This is most certainly true," as in the explanations to the Apostles' Creed and the meaning of *Amen* in the Lord's Prayer.

4. What then is the significance of such a baptism with water?

Answer: It signifies that daily the old person in us with all our sins and evil desires is to be drowned through sorrow for sin and repentance, and that daily a new person is to come forth and rise up to live before God in righteousness and purity forever.

Where is this written?

Answer: St. Paul says in Romans 6:3-4, "Do you not know that all of us who have been baptized into Christ Jesus were baptized into his death? Therefore we have been buried with him by baptism into death, so that, just as Christ was raised from the dead by the glory of the Father, so we too might walk in newness of life."

CONFESSION

What is confession?

Answer: Confession consists of two parts. One is that we confess our sins. The other is that we receive the absolution, that is, forgiveness, from the pastor as from God himself and by no means doubt but firmly believe that our sins are thereby forgiven before God in heaven.

Which sins is a person to confess?

Before God one is to acknowledge the guilt for all sins, even those of which we are not aware, as we do in the Lord's Prayer. However, before the pastor we are to confess only those sins of which we are aware and which trouble us.

Which sins are these?

Here reflect on your place in life in light of the Ten Commandments: whether you are father, mother, son, daughter, employer, employee; whether you have been disobedient, unfaithful, lazy; whether you have harmed anyone by word or deed; whether you have stolen, neglected, wasted, or injured anything.

Individual Confession and Forgiveness*

The confession made by a penitent is protected from disclosure. The pastor is obligated to respect at all times the confidential nature of a confession.

The pastor greets the penitent. When the penitent has knelt, the pastor begins:

Pastor: Are you prepared to make your confession?

Response: I am.

The pastor and penitent say the psalm together.

O Lord, open my lips,
    and my mouth shall declare your praise.
Had you desired it, I would have offered sacrifice,
    but you take no delight in burnt offerings.
The sacrifice of God is a troubled spirit;
    a broken and contrite heart, O God,
    you will not despise.
Have mercy on me, O God,
    according to your lovingkindness;
    in your great compassion blot out my offenses.
Wash me through and through from my wickedness,
    and cleanse me from my sin.

Psalm 51: 16-18, 1-2

---

* This service of individual confession from *Lutheran Book of Worship* replaces the form used in Luther's day.

Pastor: You have come to make confession before God. In Christ you are free to confess before me, a pastor in his Church, the sins of which you are aware and the sins which trouble you.

Response: I confess before God that I am guilty of many sins. Especially I confess before you that...*

*The penitent confesses those sins which are known and those which disturb or grieve him/her.***

For all this I am sorry and I pray for forgiveness. I want to do better.

* An early version of Luther's Small Catechism prepared especially for school children suggests a student might say, "As a student I have not performed my duties diligently. For I have not always done the daily work my teachers have assigned, but have often angered and offended them with my negligence, so that they have had to reprimand me because I have not cared about my studies. I also confess that I have spoken and acted indecently, have often become angry with my peers, have often complained about my teachers, and the like."

** At this point Luther reminds us: "If some individuals do not find themselves burdened by these or greater sins, they are not to worry, nor are they to search for or invent further sins and thereby turn confession into torture. Instead mention one or two that you are aware of and let that be enough. If you are aware of no sins at all (which is really quite unlikely), then do not mention any in particular, but instead receive forgiveness on the basis of the general confession that you made to God in the pastor's presence."

The pastor may then engage the penitent in pastoral conversation, offering admonition and comfort from the Holy Scriptures. Then they say together:

Have mercy on me, O God,
    according to your lovingkindness;
    in your great compassion blot out my offenses.
Create in me a clean heart, O God,
    and renew a right spirit within me.
Cast me not away from your presence,
    and take not your Holy Spirit from me.
Restore to me the joy of your salvation,
    and uphold me with your free Spirit.

Psalm 51:1, 11-13

The pastor stands and faces the penitent or remains seated and turns toward the penitent.

Pastor: Do you believe that the word of forgiveness I speak to you comes from God himself?

Response: Yes, I believe.

The pastor lays both hands on the head of the penitent.

Pastor: God is merciful and blesses you. By the command of our Lord Jesus Christ, I, a called and ordained servant of the Word, forgive you your sins in the name of the Father, and of the ✠ Son, and of the Holy Spirit.

Response: Amen.

The penitent may pray silently in thanksgiving, or may pray together with the pastor.*

---

* Luther adds, "A pastor, by using additional passages of Scripture, will in fact be able to comfort and encourage to faith those whose consciences are heavily burdened or who are distressed and under attack."

The Lord is full of compassion and mercy,
    slow to anger and of great kindness.
He will not always accuse us,
    nor will he keep his anger forever.
He has not dealt with us according to our sins,
    nor rewarded us according to our wickedness.
For as the heavens are high above the earth,
    so is his mercy great upon those who fear him.
As far as the east is from the west,
    so far has he removed our sins from us.
As a father cares for his children,
    so does the Lord care for those who fear him.

Psalm 103:8-13

Glory to the Father, and to the ✠ Son, and to the Holy Spirit; as it was in the beginning, is now, and will be forever. Amen.

Pastor: Blessed are those whose sins have been forgiven, whose evil deeds have been forgotten. Rejoice in the Lord, and go in peace.

THE SACRAMENT OF HOLY COMMUNION

1. What is the Sacrament of the Altar?

Answer: It is the true body and blood of our Lord Jesus Christ under the bread and wine, instituted by Christ himself for us Christians to eat and to drink.

Where is this written?

Answer: The holy evangelists, Matthew, Mark and Luke, and St. Paul write thus:

In the night
    in which he was betrayed,
    our Lord Jesus took bread,
    and gave thanks; broke it,
    and gave it to his disciples,
    saying: Take and eat;
    this is my body, given for you.
Do this for the remembrance of me.
Again, after supper,
    he took the cup, gave thanks,
    and gave it for all to drink,
    saying: This cup is
    the new covenant* in my blood,
    shed for you and for all people
    for the forgiveness of sin.
Do this for the remembrance of me.

* Covenant means "promise."

*2. What is the benefit of such eating and
drinking?*

Answer: The words "given for you" and "shed for
you... for the forgiveness of sin" show us that forgiveness of sin, life, and salvation are given to us in
the sacrament through these words, because where
there is forgiveness of sins, there is also life and salvation.

*3. How can bodily eating and drinking do such a
great thing?*

Answer: Eating and drinking certainly do not do it,
but rather the words that are recorded: "given for
you" and "shed for you... for the forgiveness of
sin." These words, when accompanied by the physical eating and drinking, are the essential thing in
the sacrament, and whoever believes in these very
words has what they declare and state, namely,
"forgiveness of sin."

4. Who, then, receives this sacrament worthily?

Answer: Fasting and bodily preparation are in fact
a fine external discipline, but a person who has
faith in these words, "given for you" and "shed for
you... for the forgiveness of sin," is really worthy
and well prepared. However, a person who does not
believe these words or doubts them is unworthy
and unprepared, because the words "for you"
require truly believing hearts.

MORNING AND EVENING PRAYER

How the head of the house is to teach the members of the household to say morning and evening blessings.

The Morning Blessing

In the morning, as soon as you get out of bed, you are to make the sign of the holy cross and say:

Under the care of God the Father, ✠ Son, and Holy Spirit. Amen.

Then, kneeling or standing, say the Apostles' Creed and the Lord's Prayer. If you wish, you may recite this little prayer as well:

I give thanks to you, my heavenly Father, through Jesus Christ your dear Son, that you have protected me through the night from all harm and danger and I ask that you would also protect me today from sin and every danger, so that my life and actions may please you. Into your hands I commend my body, my soul, and all that is mine. Let your holy angel be with me, so that the wicked foe may have no power over me. Amen.

After singing a hymn, or whatever else may serve your devotion, you are to go to your work joyfully.

The Evening Blessing

In the evening, when you go to bed, you are to make the sign of the holy cross and say:

> Under the care of God the Father, ✠ Son, and Holy Spirit. Amen.

Then, kneeling or standing, say the Apostles' Creed and the Lord's Prayer. If you wish, you may recite this little prayer as well:

> I give thanks to you, my heavenly Father, through Jesus Christ your dear Son, that you have graciously protected me today, and I ask you to forgive me all my sins, where I have done wrong, and graciously to protect me tonight. For into your hands I commend myself: my body, my soul, and all that is mine. Let your holy angel be with me, so that the wicked foe may have no power over me. Amen.

Then you are to go to sleep quickly and cheerfully.

BLESSINGS AT MEALS

How the head of the house is to teach members of the household to offer blessing and thanksgiving at meals.

The Table Blessing

The children and the members of the household are to come devoutly to the table, fold their hands, and recite:

> The eyes of all look to you, and you give them their food in due season. You open your hand, satisfying the desire of every living thing.*

> *Psalm 145:15-16*

---

* Luther translates this last line, "satisfies every living thing with delight," and adds that "delight" means that all animals receive enough to eat to make them joyful and of good cheer, because human worry and greed prevent such delight.

Then they are to recite the Lord's Prayer and the following prayer:

Lord God, heavenly Father, bless us and these your gifts, which we receive from your bountiful goodness through Jesus Christ our Lord. Amen.

Thanksgiving

Similarly, after eating they should in the same manner fold their hands and recite devoutly:

Praise the Lord! O give thanks to the Lord, for he is good, for his steadfast love endures forever. He gives to the animals their food, and to the young ravens when they cry. His delight is not in the strength of the horse, nor his pleasure in the speed of a runner; but the Lord takes pleasure in those who fear him, in those who hope in his steadfast love.

Psalm 106:1; 136:1,26; 147:9-11

Then recite the Lord's Prayer and the following prayer:

We give thanks to you, Lord God our Father, through Jesus Christ our Lord for all your benefits, you who live and reign forever. Amen.

A CHART OF SOME
BIBLE PASSAGES
FOR THE HOUSEHOLD*

Through these verses all kinds of holy orders and estates may be admonished, as through lessons particularly pertinent to their office and duty.

For Bishops, Pastors, and Preachers**

> Now a bishop must be above reproach, married only once, temperate, sensible, respectable, hospitable, an apt teacher, not a drunkard, not violent but gentle, not quarrelsome, and not a lover of money.
>
> *1 Timothy 3:2-3*

---

* For Martin Luther the death and resurrection of Jesus Christ, to which we are joined in our baptisms, frees us from having to impress God with who we are or what we do. By faith in God's promise in Christ we are free to serve our neighbor, not by escaping from this world to live among "religious" people, but by living our everyday lives. Thus Luther calls daily life a "holy order and estate." He divides life up into three arenas: church, society, and household. This last arena includes what we call the workplace, since in Luther's day most people lived and worked in the same place. He uses Bible verses in what has traditionally been called a "Table of Duties" to suggest how Christians may behave in various "offices" in these three arenas.

Concerning Governing Authorities***

Let every person be subject to the governing authorities; for there is no authority except from God, and those authorities that exist have been instituted by God. Therefore whoever resists authority resists what God has appointed, and those who resist will incur judgment. ...It is the servant of God to execute wrath on the wrongdoer.

Romans 13:1-2,4b

Later, Lutherans added material to describe how congregational members ought to treat their pastors and how citizens should behave in society. These biblical references are included in the following notes.

** For the duties of Christians toward their pastors and teachers, see 1 Corinthians 9:14; Galatians 6:6-7; 1 Timothy 5:17-18; 1 Thessalonians 5:12-13; Hebrews 13:7.

*** For the duties of Christians toward their government, see Matthew 22:21; Romans 13:1, 5-7; 1 Timothy 2:1-2; Titus 3:1; and 1 Peter 2:13-14.

*For Husbands**

Husbands, in the same way, show consideration for your wives in your life together, paying honor to the woman as the weaker sex, since they too are also heirs of the gracious gift of life—so that nothing may hinder your prayers.

1 Peter 3:7

Husbands, love your wives and never treat them harshly.

Colossians 3:19

---

* This section for husbands and wives is very difficult for us to understand because in our times the relation between men and women is understood differently than in Luther's day. The following suggestions may help you as you read these passages from the Bible.

◆ In Luther's day everyone, male and female, lived under the authority of someone else. The commoner was under a local lord, the city under the territorial prince, a prince under the emperor. Even the emperor was subject at that time to the parliament and imperial law. To be under someone's authority did not make you less human, nor did it give the one with authority any right to abuse you.

◆ Luther understood that relations between men and women change throughout history. Thus he reminded his own congregation that although women were thought of as property in Old Testament times, such was no longer the case. In our own time most people now support equality between the sexes, as Luther does in explaining the Sixth Commandment.

For Wives

> Wives, in the same way, accept the authority of your husbands, so that, even if some of them do not obey the word, they may be won over without a word by their wives' conduct. ...Thus Sarah obeyed Abraham and called him lord. You have become her daughters as long as you do what is good and never let fears alarm you.
>
> *1 Peter 3:1,6*

◆ As a pastor in Wittenberg Luther was very concerned that husbands not mistreat their wives. Thus he most likely understood the term "weaker sex" simply in terms of differences in brute strength. He also adds the reference to Colossians 3:19 to exclude any mistreatment of women and includes the last part of 1 Peter 3:6 to make it clear that women should not have to live in fear.

◆ The fact that husbands are asked to honor and love their wives does not exclude wives from honoring and loving their husbands. In the same way husbands are not excluded from accepting the authority of their wives.

◆ If we were compiling such a chart today, we might include Galatians 3:28 to remind us that in Christ God shows no favorites, 1 Corinthians 7:3-4 to show that there should be no sexual exploitation in marriage, and Ephesians 5:21 to remind us that all Christians should serve, love, and respect one another.

◆ What remains true is this: each and every Christian has the "office and duty" to love and serve their neighbors in whatever arena of life they find themselves.

For Parents

> And, parents, do not provoke your children to anger, but bring them up in the discipline and instruction of the Lord.

based on Ephesians 6:4

For Children

> Children, obey your parents in the Lord, for this is right. "Honor your father and mother" —this is the first commandment with a promise: "so that it may be well with you and you may live long on the earth."

Ephesians 6:1-3

For Employees*

> You employees, be obedient to your bosses with respect and cooperation, with singleness of heart, as to Christ himself; not with service meant only for the eyes, done as people-pleasers, but rather as servants of Christ, so that you do the will of God from the heart [with a good attitude]. Imagine to yourselves that you are serving the Lord and not people, and know that whatever good anyone does, the same will that person receive, whether servant or free.

based on Ephesians 6:5-8

---

*As Luther did in his day, we have altered this section to reflect the economic realities of our day and age, following Luther's own translation of this text.

For Employers

And, bosses, do the same to them. Stop
threatening them, for you know that both of
you have the same Master in heaven, and with
him there is no partiality.

based on Ephesians 6:9

For Young People in General

In the same way, you who are younger must
accept the authority of the elders. And all of
you must clothe yourselves with humility in
your dealings with one another, for "God
opposes the proud, but gives grace to the
humble." Humble yourselves therefore under
the mighty hand of God, so that he may exalt
you in due time.

1 Peter 5:5-6

For Widows

The real widow, left alone, has set her hope on
God and continues in supplications and
prayers night and day; but the widow who
lives for pleasure is dead even while she lives.

1 Timothy 5:5-6

For All in the Community

> The commandments ...are summed up in
> this word, "Love your neighbor as yourself."
>
> *Romans 13:9*

> First of all, then, I urge that supplications,
> prayers, intercessions, and thanksgivings be
> made for everyone.
>
> *1 Timothy 2:1*

Let all their lessons learn with care,
So that the household well may fare.

THE MARRIAGE SERVICE

Martin Luther's Introduction

"So many lands, so many customs," says the common proverb. For this reason, because weddings and the married estate are worldly affairs, it behooves those of us who are pastors and serve the church in no way to order or direct anything regarding marriage, but instead to allow every city and land to continue their own customs that are now in use. Some bring the bride to the church twice, in both the evening and the morning, some only once. Some announce it publicly and publish the banns from the pulpit two or three weeks in advance. All these and similar things I leave to the prince and town council to create and arrange as they want. It is no concern of mine.

---

* Every edition of the Small Catechism published during Luther's lifetime included the *Marriage Booklet*. He probably allowed this because in his day almost all households came into existence because of a marriage. We include here Luther's introduction and, in place of Luther's own marriage service (found in *Luther's Works* 53:110-115), the one from *Lutheran Book of Worship*.

However, when people request of us to bless them in front of the church or in the church, to pray over them, or even to marry them, we owe it to them to do this.* Therefore I wanted to offer this order and word of advice for those who do not know anything better, in case they are inclined to use this common order with us. Others, who can do better (that is, who can do nothing at all and who nevertheless think they know it all), do not need this service of mine, unless they might greatly improve on it and masterfully correct it. They certainly ought to take great care not to follow the same practice as others. A person might think that they had learned something from someone else! Wouldn't that be a shame?

Because up to now people have made such a big display at the consecrations of monks and nuns (even though their estate and existence is an ungodly, human invention without any basis in the Bible) how much more should we honor this godly estate of marriage and bless it, pray for it, and adorn it in an even more glorious manner.** For, although it is a worldly estate, nevertheless it has God's Word on its side and is not a human invention or institution, like the estate of monks and nuns. Therefore it should easily be reckoned a hundred times more spiritual than the monastic estate, which certainly

---

*In Luther's day the legal ceremony, consisting of the vows between the man and the woman, took place at the door of the church and the blessing was performed at the altar.

** In Luther's day many people wrongly thought that marriage was not as pleasing to God as becoming a monk or nun and imagined that such a "religious" life provided a holy escape from the drudgery and sinfulness of ordinary married life.

ought to be considered the most worldly and fleshly of all, because it was invented and instituted by flesh and blood and completely out of worldly understanding and reason.

We must also do this in order that the young people may learn to take this estate seriously, to hold it in high esteem as a divine work and command, and not to ridicule it in such outrageous ways with laughing, jeering, and similar levity. This has been common until now, as if it were a joke or child's play to get married or to have a wedding. Those who first instituted the custom of bringing a bride and bridegroom to church surely did not view it as a joke but as a very serious matter. For there is no doubt that they wanted to receive God's blessing and the common prayers and not put on a comedy or a pagan farce.

The ceremony itself makes this clear. For all who desire prayer and blessing from the pastor or bishop indicate thereby—whether or not they say so expressly—to what danger and need they are exposing themselves and how much they need God's blessing and the common prayers for the estate into which they are entering. For we experience every day how much unhappiness the devil causes in the married estate through adultery, unfaithfulness, discord, and all kinds of misery.

The Marriage Service

The bride, groom, and wedding party stand in front of the minister.

Pastor: The grace of our Lord Jesus Christ, the love of God, and the communion of the Holy Spirit be with you all.

Congregation: And also with you.

Pastor: Let us pray.

Eternal God, our creator and redeemer, as you gladdened the wedding at Cana in Galilee by the presence of your Son, so by his presence now bring your joy to this wedding. Look in favor upon _name_ and _name_ and grant that they, rejoicing in all your gifts, may at length celebrate with Christ the marriage feast which has no end.

Congregation: Amen.

One or more lessons from the Bible may be read. An address may follow. A hymn may be sung.

Pastor: The Lord God in his goodness created us male and female, and by the gift of marriage founded human community in a joy that begins now and is brought to perfection in the life to come.

Because of sin, our age-old rebellion, the gladness of marriage can be overcast and the gift of the family can become a burden. But because God, who

established marriage, continues still to bless it with
his abundant and ever-present support, we can be
sustained in our weariness and have our joy
restored.

Pastor: _name_ and _name_ , if it is your intention
to share with each other your joys and sorrows and
all that the years will bring, with your promises bind
yourselves to each other as husband and wife.

*The bride and groom face each other and join
hands.*

I take you, _name_ ,
to be my wife/husband from this day forward,
to join with you and share all that is to come,
and I promise to be faithful to you
until death parts us.

*The bride and groom exchange rings with these
words:*

I give you this ring as a sign of my love and
faithfulness.

The bride and groom join hands.

Pastor: _name_ and _name_ , by their promises before
God and in the presence of this congregation, have
bound themselves to one another as husband and
wife.

Congregation: Blessed be the Father and the Son and
the Holy Spirit now and forever.

Pastor: Those whom God has joined together let no one put asunder.

Congregation: Amen.

The bride and groom kneel.

Pastor: The Lord God, who created our first parents and established them in marriage, establish and sustain you, that you may find delight in each other and grow in holy love until your life's end.

Congregation: Amen.

The parents may add their blessing with these or similar words; the wedding party may join them.

May you dwell in God's presence forever; may true and constant love preserve you.

Pastor: Let us bless God for all gifts in which we rejoice today.

Lord God, constant in mercy, great in faithfulness: With high praise we recall your acts of unfailing love for the human family, for the house of Israel, and for your people the Church.

We bless you for the joy which your servants, ___name___ and ___name___ , have found in each other, and pray that you give to us such a sense of your constant love that we may employ all our strength in a life of praise of you, whose work alone holds true and endures forever.

Congregation: Amen.

Pastor: Let us pray for ___name___ and ___name___ in their life together.

Faithful Lord, source of love, pour down your grace upon ___name___ and ___name___ , that they may fulfill the vows they have made this day and reflect your steadfast love in their life-long faithfulness to each other; and from your great store of strength give them power and patience, affection and understanding, courage, and love toward you, toward each other, and toward the world, that they may continue together in mutual growth according to your will in Jesus Christ our Lord.

Congregation: Amen.

When Holy Communion is celebrated, the service continues with the Peace. When there is no Communion, the service continues with the Lord's Prayer.

Pastor: Almighty God, Father, ✠ Son, and Holy Spirit, keep you in his light and truth and love now and forever.

Congregation: Amen.

THE SERVICE OF HOLY BAPTISM*

Martin Luther's Introduction

To all Christian readers:

Grace and peace in Christ our Lord.

Because daily I see and hear with what careless-
ness and lack of solemnity—to say nothing of out
and out levity—people treat the high, holy, and

---

*The Marriage service defines the household in relation to God's creation. Holy
Baptism defines members of that household in relation to God's grace in Jesus
Christ. We include here Luther's introduction to his own translation of the baptismal service and the service for Holy Baptism from *Lutheran Book of Worship*
(using the wording for baptism of children). The "flood prayer" in our service is
adapted from Luther's *Baptismal Booklet*.

Two important aspects of the *Baptismal Booklet* are not in our service. First,
the ancient service of Holy Baptism that Luther translated from the Latin also
included a section in which the pastor meets the baptismal party at the door of the
church and commands the devil to leave the child alone. This was not mere super-
stition, but a clear confession by Luther of the evil in which we all live and of the
power of God to use Holy Baptism and its promises to rescue us. It is because of
God's act in defeating evil on the cross that we can renounce "all the forces of evil,
the devil, and all his empty promises." In Holy Baptism Christ's victory over sin,
death, and the devil is applied to us. Luther's conviction that this is true shapes his
entire introduction. Second, Luther's service included the reading of Mark 10:13-
16, which describes Jesus' blessing of the small children. This helped remind his
hearers that Holy Baptism is not something adults do for God, but rather something the Holy Spirit does to us through the water and the Word, no matter what
our age, in order that we may trust in God and not in ourselves.

comforting Sacrament of Baptism for infants, in part caused, I believe, by the fact that those present understand nothing of what is being said and done, I have decided that it is not only helpful but also necessary to conduct the service in the German language. For this reason I have translated those portions that used to be said in Latin in order to begin baptizing in German, so that the sponsors and others present may be all the more aroused to faith and earnest devotion and so that the pastors who baptize have to show more diligence for the sake of the listeners.

Out of a sense of Christian commitment, I appeal to all those who baptize, sponsor infants, or witness a baptism to take to heart the tremendous work and great solemnity present here. For here in the words of these prayers you hear how plaintively and earnestly the Christian church brings the infant to God, confesses before him with such unchanging, undoubting words that the infant is possessed by the devil and a child of sin and wrath, and so diligently asks for help and grace through Baptism, that the infant may become a child of God.

Therefore, you need to consider that it is no joke at all to take action against the devil and not only drive him away from the little child but also hang around its neck such a mighty, lifelong enemy. Thus it is extremely necessary to stand by the poor child with all your heart and with a strong faith and to plead with great devotion that God, in accordance with these prayers, would not only free the child from the devil's power but also strengthen the child, so that the child might resist him like a fighter in life and in death. I fear that people turn out so badly after Baptism because we have dealt with them in such a cold and casual way and have prayed for them at their baptism without any zeal at all.

Bear in mind, too, that in Baptism the external ceremonies are least important, such as blowing under the eyes, making the sign of the cross, putting salt in the mouth or spit and clay in the ears and nose, anointing the breast and shoulders with oil, smearing the head with chrism, putting on the christening robe, placing a burning candle in the child's hand, and whatever else has been added by humans to embellish Baptism. For certainly a baptism can occur without any of these things, and they are not the proper devices from which the devil shrinks or flees. He sneers at even greater things than these! Here things must get really serious.

Instead, see to it that you are present there in true faith, that you listen to God's Word, and that you pray along earnestly. For wherever the pastors say, "Let us pray," they are exhorting you to pray with them. Moreover, all sponsors and the others present ought to speak along with them the words of their prayers in their hearts to God. For this reason, the pastors should speak these prayers very clearly and slowly, so that the sponsors can hear and understand them and can also pray with the pastors with one mind in their hearts, carrying before God the need of the little child with all earnestness, on the child's behalf setting themselves against the devil with all their strength, and demonstrating that they take seriously what is no joke to the devil.

For this reason it is right and proper not to allow drunken and boorish pastors to baptize nor to select loose people as godparents. Instead fine, moral, serious, upright pastors and godparents ought to be chosen, who can be expected to treat the matter with seriousness and true faith, lest this high sacrament be abandoned to the devil's mockery and dishonor God, who in this sacrament showers upon us the vast and boundless riches of his grace. He himself calls it a "new birth," through which we, being freed from the devil's tyranny and loosed from sin, death, and hell, become children of life, heirs of all God's possessions, God's own children, and brothers and sisters of Christ.

Ah, dear Christians, let us not value and treat this unspeakable gift so half-heartedly. For Baptism is our only comfort and doorway to all of God's possessions and to the communion of all the saints. To this end may God help us. Amen.

The Service of Holy Baptism

The minister addresses the baptismal group and the congregation.

Pastor: In Holy Baptism our gracious heavenly Father liberates us from sin and death by joining us to the death and resurrection of our Lord Jesus Christ. We are born children of a fallen humanity; in the waters of Baptism we are reborn children of God and inheritors of eternal life. By water and the Holy Spirit we are made members of the Church which is the body of Christ. As we live with him and with his people, we grow in faith, love, and obedience to the will of God.

A sponsor for each candidate presents the candidate:

I present ___name___ to receive the Sacrament of Holy Baptism.

The minister addresses the sponsors and parents.

Pastor: In Christian love you have presented these children for Holy Baptism. You should, therefore, faithfully bring them to the services of God's house, and teach them the Lord's Prayer, the Creed, and the Ten Commandments. As they grow in years, you should place in their hands the Holy Scriptures and provide for their instruction in the Christian faith, that, living in the covenant of their Baptism and in communion with the Church, they may lead godly lives until the day of Jesus Christ.

Do you promise to fulfill these obligations?

Response: I do.

Pastor: The Lord be with you.

Congregation: And also with you.

Pastor: Let us give thanks to the Lord our God.

Congregation: It is right to give him thanks and praise.

Pastor: Holy God, mighty Lord, gracious Father: We give you thanks, for in the beginning your Spirit moved over the waters and you created heaven and earth. By the gift of water you nourish and sustain us and all living things.

By the waters of the flood you condemned the wicked and saved those whom you had chosen, Noah and his family. You led Israel by the pillar of cloud and fire through the sea, out of slavery into the freedom of the promised land. In the waters of the Jordan your Son was baptized by John and anointed with the Spirit. By the baptism of his own death and resurrection your beloved Son has set us free from the bondage to sin and death, and has opened the way to the joy and freedom of everlasting life. He made water a sign of the kingdom and of cleansing and rebirth. In obedience to his command, we make disciples of all nations, baptizing them in the name of the Father, and of the Son, and of the Holy Spirit.

Pour out your Holy Spirit, so that those who are here baptized may be given new life. Wash away the sin of all those who are cleansed by this water and bring them forth as inheritors of your glorious kingdom.

To you be given praise and honor and worship through your Son, Jesus Christ our Lord, in the unity of the Holy Spirit, now and forever. Amen.

The minister addresses the people.

Pastor: I ask you to profess your faith in Christ Jesus, reject sin, and confess the faith of the Church, the faith in which we baptize.

Pastor: Do you renounce all the forces of evil, the devil, and all his empty promises?

Congregation: I do.

Pastor: Do you believe in God the Father?

Congregation: I believe in God, the Father almighty, creator of heaven and earth.

Pastor: Do you believe in Jesus Christ, the Son of God?

Congregation: I believe in Jesus Christ, his only Son, our Lord.
He was conceived by the power of the Holy Spirit
and born of the virgin Mary.
He suffered under Pontius Pilate,
was crucified, died, and was buried.
He descended into hell.
On the third day he rose again.
He ascended into heaven,
and is seated at the right hand of the Father.
He will come again to judge the living and the dead.

Pastor: Do you believe in God the Holy Spirit?

Congregation: I believe in the Holy Spirit,
the holy catholic Church,
the communion of saints,
the forgiveness of sins,
the resurrection of the body,
and the life everlasting. Amen.

The minister baptizes each candidate by pouring water on the head.

Pastor: name , I baptize you in the name of the Father, and of the Son, and of the Holy Spirit. Amen.

Pastor: The Lord be with you.

Congregation: And also with you.

Pastor: God, the Father of our Lord Jesus Christ, we give you thanks for freeing your sons and daughters from the power of sin and for raising them up to a new life through this holy sacrament. Pour your Holy Spirit upon name : the spirit of wisdom and understanding, the spirit of counsel and might, the spirit of knowledge and the fear of the Lord, the spirit of joy in your presence.

Congregation: Amen.

The minister marks the sign of the cross on the fore-head of each of the baptized. Oil prepared for this purpose may be used.

Pastor: __name__ , child of God, you have been sealed by the Holy Spirit and marked with the cross of Christ forever.

A lighted candle may be given to each of the baptized by a representative of the congregation who says:

Let your light so shine before others that they may see your good works and glorify your Father in heaven.

When small children are baptized, this prayer may be said.

Pastor: O God, the giver of all life, look with kindness upon the fathers and mothers of these children. Let them ever rejoice in the gift you have given them. Make them teachers and examples of righteousness for their children. Strengthen them in their own Baptism so they may share eternally with their children the salvation you have given them, through Jesus Christ our Lord. Amen.

A representative of the congregation says:

Through Baptism God has made these new sisters and brothers members of the priesthood we all share in Christ Jesus, that we may proclaim the praise of God and bear his creative and redeeming Word to all the world.

Congregation: We welcome you into the Lord's family. We receive you as fellow members of the body of Christ, children of the same heavenly Father, and workers with us in the kingdom of God.

All exchange the peace.

THE
REVISED COMMON
LECTIONARY

Year A

First Sunday in Advent
Isaiah 2:1-5
Psalm 122
Romans 13:11-14
Matthew 24:36-44

Second Sunday in Advent
Isaiah 11:1-10
Psalm 72:1-7, 18-19
Romans 15:4-13
Matthew 3:1-12

Third Sunday in Advent
Isaiah 35:1-10
Psalm 146:4-9
James 5:7-10
Matthew 11:2-11

Fourth Sunday in Advent
Isaiah 7:10-16
Psalm 80:1-7, 16-18
(80:1-7, 17-19 NRSV)
Romans 1:1-7
Matthew 1:18-25

Christmas Eve (I)
Isaiah 9:2-7
Psalm 96
Titus 2:11-14
Luke 2:1-14 [15-20]

Christmas Dawn (II)
Isaiah 62:6-12
Psalm 97
Titus 3:4-7
Luke 2:[1-7] 8-20

Christmas Day (III)
Isaiah 52:7-10
Psalm 98
Hebrews 1:1-4 [5-12]
John 1:1-14

*First Sunday after
Christmas*
Isaiah 63:7-9
Psalm 148
Hebrews 2:10-18
Matthew 2:13-23

Second Sunday after
Christmas
Jeremiah 31:7-14
Psalm 147:13-21
(147:12-20 NRSV)
Ephesians 1:3-14
John 1:[1-9] 10-18

The Epiphany of Our Lord
Isaiah 60:1-6
Psalm 72:1-7, 10-14
Ephesians 3:1-12
Matthew 2:1-12

The Baptism of Our Lord
(First Sunday after the
Epiphany)
Isaiah 42:1-9
Psalm 29
Acts 10:34-43
Matthew 3:13-17

Second Sunday after the
Epiphany
Isaiah 49:1-7
Psalm 40:1-12
1 Corinthians 1:1-9
John 1:29-42

Third Sunday after the
Epiphany
Isaiah 9:1-4
Psalm 27:1, 5-13
(27:1, 4-9 NRSV)
1 Corinthians 1:10-18
Matthew 4:12-23

Fourth Sunday after the
Epiphany
Micah 6:1-8
Psalm 15
1 Corinthians 1:18-31
Matthew 5:1-12

Fifth Sunday after the
Epiphany
Isaiah 58:1-9a [9b-12]
Psalm 112:1-9 [10]
1 Corinthians 2:1-12 [13-
16]
Matthew 5:13-20

Sixth Sunday after the
Epiphany
Deuteronomy 30:15-20
Psalm 119:1-8
1 Corinthians 3:1-9
Matthew 5:21-37

Seventh Sunday after the
Epiphany
Leviticus 19:1-2, 9-18
Psalm 119:33-40
1 Corinthians 3:10-11,
16-23
Matthew 5:38-48

Eighth Sunday after the
Epiphany
Isaiah 49:8-16a
Psalm 131
1 Corinthians 4:1-5
Matthew 6:24-34

*The Transfiguration of Our
Lord (Last Sunday after the
Epiphany)*
Exodus 24:12-18
Psalm 2
2 Peter 1:16-21
Matthew 17:1-9

Ash Wednesday
Joel 2:1-2, 12-17
Psalm 51:1-18
(51:1-17 NRSV)
2 Corinthians 5:20b—6:10
Matthew 6:1-6, 16-21

First Sunday in Lent
Genesis 2:15-17; 3:1-7
Psalm 32
Romans 5:12-19
Matthew 4:1-11

Second Sunday in Lent
Genesis 12:1-4a
Psalm 121
Romans 4:1-5, 13-17
John 3:1-17

Third Sunday in Lent
Exodus 17:1-7
Psalm 95
Romans 5:1-11
John 4:5-42

Fourth Sunday in Lent
1 Samuel 16:1-13
Psalm 23
Ephesians 5:8-14
John 9:1-41

Fifth Sunday in Lent
Ezekiel 37:1-14
Psalm 130
Romans 8:6-11
John 11:1-45

*Sunday of the Passion /
Palm Sunday: Liturgy of
the Passion*
Isaiah 50:4-9a
Psalm 31:9-16
Philippians 2:5-11
Matthew 26:14—27:66

Monday in Holy Week
Isaiah 42:1-9
Psalm 36:5-11
Hebrews 9:11-15
John 12:1-11

Tuesday in Holy Week
Isaiah 49:1-7
Psalm 71:1-14
1 Corinthians 1:18-31
John 12:20-36

Wednesday in Holy Week
Isaiah 50:4-9a
Psalm 70
Hebrews 12:1-3
John 13:21-32

Maundy Thursday
Exodus 12:1-4 [5-10] 11-14
Psalm 116:1, 10-17
(116:1-2, 12-19 NRSV)
1 Corinthians 11:23-26
John 13:1-17, 31b-35

Good Friday
Isaiah 52:13—53:12
Psalm 22
Hebrews 10:16-25
John 18:1—19:42

The Resurrection of Our Lord: Vigil of Easter
Genesis 1:1-2:4a
Genesis 7:1-5, 11-18; 8:6-18; 9:8-13
Genesis 22:1-18
Exodus 14:10-31; 15:20-21
Isaiah 55:1-11
Proverbs 8:1-8, 19-21; 9:4b-6
Ezekiel 36:24-28
Ezekiel 37:1-14
Zephaniah 3:14-20
Jonah 3:1-10
Deuteronomy 31:19-30
Daniel 3:1-29
Romans 6:3-11
Matthew 28:1-10

The Resurrection of Our Lord: Easter Day
Acts 10:34-43
Psalm 118:1-2, 14-24
Colossians 3:1-4
John 20:1-18

The Resurrection of Our Lord: Easter Evening
Isaiah 25:6-9
Psalm 114
1 Corinthians 5:6b-8
Luke 24:13-49

Second Sunday of Easter
Acts 2:14a, 22-32
Psalm 16
1 Peter 1:3-9
John 20:19-31

Third Sunday of Easter
Acts 2:14a, 36-41
Psalm 116:1-3, 10-17
(116:1-4, 12-19 NRSV)
1 Peter 1:17-23
Luke 24:13-35

Fourth Sunday of Easter
Acts 2:42-47
Psalm 23
1 Peter 2:19-25
John 10:1-10

Fifth Sunday of Easter
Acts 7:55-60
Psalm 31:1-5, 15-16
1 Peter 2:2-10
John 14:1-14

Sixth Sunday of Easter
Acts 17:22-31
Psalm 66:7-18
(66:8-20 NRSV)
1 Peter 3:13-22
John 14:15-21

The Ascension of Our Lord
Acts 1:1-11
Psalm 47
Ephesians 1:15-23
Luke 24:44-53

Seventh Sunday of Easter
Acts 1:6-14
Psalm 68:1-10, 33-36
(68:1-10, 32-35 NRSV)
1 Peter 4:12-14; 5:6-11
John 17:1-11

Vigil of Pentecost
Exodus 19:1-9
Psalm 33:12-22
Romans 8:14-17, 22-27
John 7:37-39

The Day of Pentecost
Acts 2:1-21
Psalm 104:25-35, 37
(104:24-34, 35b NRSV)
1 Corinthians 12:3b-13
John 20:19-23

*The Holy Trinity (First
Sunday after Pentecost)*
Genesis 1:1—2:4a
Psalm 8
2 Corinthians 13:11-13
Matthew 28:16-20

Proper 3
Isaiah 49:8-16a
Psalm 131
1 Corinthians 4:1-5
Matthew 6:24-34

Proper 4
Deuteronomy 11:18-21,
26-28
Psalm 31:1-5, 19-24
Romans 1:16-17; 3:22b-28
[29-31]
Matthew 7:21-29

Proper 5
Hosea 5:15—6:6
Psalm 50:7-15
Romans 4:13-25
Matthew 9:9-13, 18-26

Proper 6
Exodus 19:2-8a
Psalm 100
Romans 5:1-8
Matthew 9:35—10:8 [9-23]

Proper 7
Jeremiah 20:7-13
Psalm 69:8-11 [12-17] 18-
20 (69:7-10 [11-15] 16-18
NRSV)
Romans 6:1b-11
Matthew 10:24-39

Proper 8
Jeremiah 28:5-9
Psalm 89:1-4, 15-18
Romans 6:12-23
Matthew 10:40-42

Proper 9
Zechariah 9:9-12
Psalm 145:8-15
(145:8-14 NRSV)
Romans 7:15-25a
Matthew 11:16-19, 25-30

Proper 10
Isaiah 55:10-13
Psalm 65:[1-8] 9-14
(65:[1-8] 9-13 NRSV)
Romans 8:1-11
Matthew 13:1-9, 18-23

Proper 11
Isaiah 44:6-8
Psalm 86:11-17
Romans 8:12-25
Matthew 13:24-30, 36-43

Proper 12
1 Kings 3:5-12
Psalm 119:129-136
Romans 8:26-39
Matthew 13:31-33, 44-52

Proper 13
Isaiah 55:1-5
Psalm 145:8-9, 15-22
(145:8-9, 14-21 NRSV)
Romans 9:1-5
Matthew 14:13-21

Proper 14
1 Kings 19:9-18
Psalm 85:8-13
Romans 10:5-15
Matthew 14:22-33

Proper 15
Isaiah 56:1, 6-8
Psalm 67
Romans 11:1-2a, 29-32
Matthew 15:[10-20] 21-28

Proper 16
Isaiah 51:1-6
Psalm 138
Romans 12:1-8
Matthew 16:13-20

Proper 17
Jeremiah 15:15-21
Psalm 26:1-8
Romans 12:9-21
Matthew 16:21-28

Proper 18
Ezekiel 33:7-11
Psalm 119:33-40
Romans 13:8-14
Matthew 18:15-20

Proper 19
Genesis 50:15-21
Psalm 103:[1-7] 8-13
Romans 14:1-12
Matthew 18:21-35

Proper 20
Jonah 3:10—4:11
Psalm 145:1-8
Philippians 1:21-30
Matthew 20:1-16

Proper 21
Ezekiel 18:1-4, 25-32
Psalm 25:1-8
(25:1-9 NRSV)
Philippians 2:1-13
Matthew 21:23-32

Proper 22
Isaiah 5:1-7
Psalm 80:7-14
(80:7-15 NRSV)
Philippians 3:4b-14
Matthew 21:33-46

Proper 23
Isaiah 25:1-9
Psalm 23
Philippians 4:1-9
Matthew 22:1-14

Proper 24
Isaiah 45:1-7
Psalm 96:1-9 [10-13]
1 Thessalonians 1:1-10
Matthew 22:15-22

Proper 25
Leviticus 19:1-2, 15-18
Psalm 1
1 Thessalonians 2:1-8
Matthew 22:34-46

Proper 26
Micah 3:5-12
Psalm 43
1 Thessalonians 2:9-13
Matthew 23:1-12

Proper 27
Amos 5:18-24
Psalm 70
1 Thessalonians 4:13-18
Matthew 25:1-13

Proper 28
Zephaniah 1:7, 12-18
Psalm 90:1-8 [9-11] 12
1 Thessalonians 5:1-11
Matthew 25:14-30

Christ the King
Ezekiel 34:11-16, 20-24
Psalm 95:1-7a
Ephesians 1:15-23
Matthew 25:31-46

Reformation Day
Jeremiah 31:31-34
Psalm 46
Romans 3:19-28
John 8:31-36

All Saints' Day
Revelation 7:9-17
Psalm 34:1-10, 22
1 John 3:1-3
Matthew 5:1-12

Day of Thanksgiving
Deuteronomy 8:7-18
Psalm 65
2 Corinthians 9:6-15
Luke 17:11-19

Year B

First Sunday in Advent
Isaiah 64:1-9
Psalm 80:1-7, 16-18
(80:1-7,17-19 NRSV)
1 Corinthians 1:3-9
Mark 13:24-37

Second Sunday in Advent
Isaiah 40:1-11
Psalm 85:1-2, 8-13
2 Peter 3:8-15a
Mark 1:1-8

Third Sunday in Advent
Isaiah 61:1-4, 8-11
Psalm 126
1 Thessalonians 5:16-24
John 1:6-8, 19-28

Fourth Sunday in Advent
2 Samuel 7:1-11, 16
Luke 1:47-55
Romans 16:25-27
Luke 1:26-38

Christmas Eve (I)
Isaiah 9:2-7
Psalm 96
Titus 2:11-14
Luke 2:1-14

Christmas Dawn (II)
Isaiah 62:6-12
Psalm 97
Titus 3:4-7
Luke 2:[1-7] 8-20

Christmas Day (III)
Isaiah 52:7-10
Psalm 98
Hebrews 1:1-4 [5-12]
John 1:1-14

First Sunday after Christmas
Isaiah 61:10—62:3
Psalm 148
Galatians 4:4-7
Luke 2:22-40

Second Sunday after Christmas
Jeremiah 31:7-14
Psalm 147:13-21
(147:12-20 NRSV)
Ephesians 1:3-14
John 1:[1-9] 10-18

The Epiphany of Our Lord
Isaiah 60:1-6
Psalm 72:1-7, 10-14
Ephesians 3:1-12
Matthew 2:1-12

The Baptism of Our Lord (First Sunday after the Epiphany)
Genesis 1:1-5
Psalm 29
Acts 19:1-7
Mark 1:4-11

Second Sunday after the Epiphany
1 Samuel 3:1-10 [11-20]
Psalm 139:1-5, 12-17
(139:1-6, 13-18 NRSV)
1 Corinthians 6:12-20
John 1:43-51

Third Sunday after the Epiphany
Jonah 3:1-5, 10
Psalm 62:6-14
(62:5-12 NRSV)
1 Corinthians 7:29-31
Mark 1:14-20

Fourth Sunday after the Epiphany
Deuteronomy 18:15-20
Psalm 111
1 Corinthians 8:1-13
Mark 1:21-28

Fifth Sunday after the Epiphany
Isaiah 40:21-31
Psalm 147:1-12, 21c
(147:1-11, 20c NRSV)
1 Corinthians 9:16-23
Mark 1:29-39

*Sixth Sunday after the
Epiphany*
2 Kings 5:1-14
Psalm 30
1 Corinthians 9:24-27
Mark 1:40-45

*Seventh Sunday after the
Epiphany*
Isaiah 43:18-25
Psalm 41
2 Corinthians 1:18-22
Mark 2:1-12

*Eighth Sunday after the
Epiphany*
Hosea 2:14-20
Psalm 103:1-13, 22
2 Corinthians 3:1-6
Mark 2:13-22

*The Transfiguration of Our
Lord (Last Sunday after the
Epiphany)*
2 Kings 2:1-12
Psalm 50:1-6
2 Corinthians 4:3-6
Mark 9:2-9

Ash Wednesday
Joel 2:1-2, 12-17
Psalm 51:1-18
(51:1-17 NRSV)
2 Corinthians 5:20b—6:10
Matthew 6:1-6, 16-21

First Sunday in Lent
Genesis 9:8-17
Psalm 25:1-9
(25:1-10 NRSV)
1 Peter 3:18-22
Mark 1:9-15

Second Sunday in Lent
Genesis 17:1-7, 15-16
Psalm 22:22-30
(22:23-31 NRSV)
Romans 4:13-25
Mark 8:31-38

Third Sunday in Lent
Exodus 20:1-17
Psalm 19
1 Corinthians 1:18-25
John 2:13-22

Fourth Sunday in Lent
Numbers 21:4-9
Psalm 107:1-3, 17-22
Ephesians 2:1-10
John 3:14-21

Fifth Sunday in Lent
Jeremiah 31:31-34
Psalm 51:1-13
(51:1-12 NRSV)
Hebrews 5:5-10
John 12:20-33

*Sunday of the Passion /
Palm Sunday: Liturgy of
the Passion*
Isaiah 50:4-9a
Psalm 31:9-16
Philippians 2:5-11
Mark 14:1—15:47

Monday in Holy Week
Isaiah 42:1-9
Psalm 36:5-11
Hebrews 9:11-15
John 12:1-11

Tuesday in Holy Week
Isaiah 49:1-7
Psalm 71:1-14
1 Corinthians 1:18-31
John 12:20-36

Wednesday in Holy Week
Isaiah 50:4-9a
Psalm 70
Hebrews 12:1-3
John 13:21-32

Maundy Thursday
Exodus 12:1-4 [5-10] 11-14
Psalm 116:1, 10-17
(116:1-2, 12-19 NRSV)
1 Corinthians 11:23-26
John 13:1-17, 31b-35

Good Friday
Isaiah 52:13—53:12
Psalm 22
Hebrews 10:16-25
John 18:1—19:42

*The Resurrection of Our
Lord: Vigil of Easter*
Genesis 1:1-2:4a
Genesis 7:1-5, 11-18; 8:6-
18; 9:8-13
Genesis 22:1-18
Exodus 14:10-31; 15:20-21
Isaiah 55:1-11
Proverbs 8:1-8, 19-21;
9:4b-6
Ezekiel 36:24-28
Ezekiel 37:1-14
Zephaniah 3:14-20
Jonah 3:1-10
Deuteronomy 31:19-30
Daniel 3:1-29
Romans 6:3-11
Mark 16:1-8

*The Resurrection of Our
Lord: Easter Day*
Acts 10:34-43
Psalm 118:1-2, 14-24
1 Corinthians 15:1-11
John 20:1-18

*The Resurrection of Our
Lord: Easter Evening*
Isaiah 25:6-9
Psalm 114
1 Corinthians 5:6b-8
Luke 24:13-49

Second Sunday of Easter
Acts 4:32-35
Psalm 133
1 John 1:1—2:2
John 20:19-31

Third Sunday of Easter
Acts 3:12-19
Psalm 4
1 John 3:1-7
Luke 24:36b-48

Fourth Sunday of Easter
Acts 4:5-12
Psalm 23
1 John 3:16-24
John 10:11-18

Fifth Sunday of Easter
Acts 8:26-40
Psalm 22:24-30
(22:25-31 NRSV)
1 John 4:7-21
John 15:1-8

Sixth Sunday of Easter
Acts 10:44-48
Psalm 98
1 John 5:1-6
John 15:9-17

The Ascension of Our Lord
Acts 1:1-11
Psalm 47
Ephesians 1:15-23
Luke 24:44-53

Seventh Sunday of Easter
Acts 1:15-17, 21-26
Psalm 1
1 John 5:9-13
John 17:6-19

Vigil of Pentecost
Exodus 19:1-9
Psalm 33:12-22
Romans 8:14-17, 22-27
John 7:37-39

The Day of Pentecost
Acts 2:1-21
Psalm 104:25-35, 37
(104:24-34, 35b NRSV)
Romans 8:22-27
John 15:26-27; 16:4b-15

The Holy Trinity (First Sunday after Pentecost)
Isaiah 6:1-8
Psalm 29
Romans 8:12-17
John 3:1-17

Proper 3
Hosea 2:14-20
Psalm 103:1-13, 22
2 Corinthians 3:1-6
Mark 2:13-22

Proper 4
Deuteronomy 5:12-15
Psalm 81:1-10
2 Corinthians 4:5-12
Mark 2:23—3:6

Proper 5
Genesis 3:8-15
Psalm 130
2 Corinthians 4:13—5:1
Mark 3:20-35

Proper 6
Ezekiel 17:22-24
Psalm 92:1-4, 11-14
(92:1-4, 12-15 NRSV)
2 Corinthians 5:6-10 [11-13] 14-17
Mark 4:26-34

Proper 7
Job 38:1-11
Psalm 107:1-3, 23-32
2 Corinthians 6:1-13
Mark 4:35-41

Proper 8
Lamentations 3:22-33
Psalm 30
2 Corinthians 8:7-15
Mark 5:21-43

Proper 9
Ezekiel 2:1-5
Psalm 123
2 Corinthians 12:2-10
Mark 6:1-13

Proper 10
Amos 7:7-15
Psalm 85:8-13
Ephesians 1:3-14
Mark 6:14-29

Proper 11
Jeremiah 23:1-6
Psalm 23
Ephesians 2:11-22
Mark 6:30-34, 53-56

Proper 12
2 Kings 4:42-44
Psalm 145:10-19
(10-18 NRSV)
Ephesians 3:14-21
John 6:1-21

Proper 13
Exodus 16:2-4, 9-15
Psalm 78:23-29
Ephesians 4:1-16
John 6:24-35

Proper 14
1 Kings 19:4-8
Psalm 34:1-8
Ephesians 4:25—5:2
John 6:35, 41-51

Proper 15
Proverbs 9:1-6
Psalm 34:9-14
Ephesians 5:15-20
John 6:51-58

Proper 16
Joshua 24:1-2a, 14-18
Psalm 34:15-22
Ephesians 6:10-20
John 6:56-69

Proper 17
Deuteronomy 4:1-2, 6-9
Psalm 15
James 1:17-27
Mark 7:1-8, 14-15, 21-23

Proper 18
Isaiah 35:4-7a
Psalm 146
James 2:1-10 [11-13] 14-17
Mark 7:24-37

Proper 19
Isaiah 50:4-9a
Psalm 116:1-8
(116:1-9 NRSV)
James 3:1-12
Mark 8:27-38

Proper 20
Jeremiah 11:18-20
Psalm 54
James 3:13—4:3, 7-8a
Mark 9:30-37

Proper 21
Numbers 11:4-6, 10-16,
24-29
Psalm 19:7-14
James 5:13-20
Mark 9:38-50

Proper 22
Genesis 2:18-24
Psalm 8
Hebrews 1:1-4; 2:5-12
Mark 10:2-16

Proper 23
Amos 5:6-7, 10-15
Psalm 90:12-17
Hebrews 4:12-16
Mark 10:17-31

Proper 24
Isaiah 53:4-12
Psalm 91:9-16
Hebrews 5:1-10
Mark 10:35-45

Proper 25
Jeremiah 31:7-9
Psalm 126
Hebrews 7:23-28
Mark 10:46-52

Proper 26
Deuteronomy 6:1-9
Psalm 119:1-8
Hebrews 9:11-14
Mark 12:28-34

Proper 27
1 Kings 17:8-16
Psalm 146
Hebrews 9:24-28
Mark 12:38-44

Proper 28
Daniel 12:1-3
Psalm 16
Hebrews 10:11-14 [15-18]
19-25
Mark 13:1-8

Christ the King
Daniel 7:9-10, 13-14
Psalm 93
Revelation 1:4b-8
John 18:33-37

Reformation Day
Jeremiah 31:31-34
Psalm 46
Romans 3:19-28
John 8:31-36

All Saints' Day
Isaiah 25:6-9
Psalm 24
Revelation 21:1-6a
John 11:32-44

Day of Thanksgiving
Joel 2:21-27
Psalm 126
1 Timothy 2:1-7
Matthew 6:25-33

Year C

First Sunday in Advent
Jeremiah 33:14-16
Psalm 25:1-9
1 Thessalonians 3:9-13
Luke 21:25-36

Second Sunday in Advent
Malachi 3:1-4
Luke 1:68-79
Philippians 1:3-11
Luke 3:1-6

Third Sunday in Advent
Zephaniah 3:14-20
Isaiah 12:2-6
Philippians 4:4-7
Luke 3:7-18

Fourth Sunday in Advent
Micah 5:2-5a
Luke 1:47-55
Hebrews 10:5-10
Luke 1:39-45 [46-55]

Christmas Eve (I)
Isaiah 9:2-7
Psalm 96
Titus 2:11-14
Luke 2:1-14 [15-20]

Christmas Dawn (II)
Isaiah 62:6-12
Psalm 97
Titus 3:4-7
Luke 2:[1-7] 8-20

Christmas Day (III)
Isaiah 52:7-10
Psalm 98
Hebrews 1:1-4 [5-12]
John 1:1-14

First Sunday after Christmas
1 Samuel 2:18-20, 26
Psalm 148
Colossians 3:12-17
Luke 2:41-52

Second Sunday after Christmas
Jeremiah 31:7-14
Psalm 147:13-21
(147:12-20 NRSV)
Ephesians 1:3-14
John 1:[1-9] 10-18

The Epiphany of Our Lord
Isaiah 60:1-6
Psalm 72:1-7, 10-14
Ephesians 3:1-12
Matthew 2:1-12

*The Baptism of Our Lord
(First Sunday after the
Epiphany)*
Isaiah 43:1-7
Psalm 29
Acts 8:14-17
Luke 3:15-17, 21-22

*Second Sunday after the
Epiphany*
Isaiah 62:1-5
Psalm 36:5-10
1 Corinthians 12:1-11
John 2:1-11

*Third Sunday after the
Epiphany*
Nehemiah 8:1-3, 5-6, 8-10
Psalm 19
1 Corinthians 12:12-31a
Luke 4:14-21

*Fourth Sunday after the
Epiphany*
Jeremiah 1:4-10
Psalm 71:1-6
1 Corinthians 13:1-13
Luke 4:21-30

Fifth Sunday after the Epiphany
Isaiah 6:1-8 [9-13]
Psalm 138
1 Corinthians 15:1-11
Luke 5:1-11

Sixth Sunday after the Epiphany
Jeremiah 17:5-10
Psalm 1
1 Corinthians 15:12-20
Luke 6:17-26

Seventh Sunday after the Epiphany
Genesis 45:3-11, 15
Psalm 37:1-12, 41-42
(37:1-11, 39-40 NRSV)
1 Corinthians 15:35-38, 42-50
Luke 6:27-38

Eighth Sunday after the Epiphany
Isaiah 55:10-13
Psalm 92:1-4, 11-14
(92:1-4, 12-15 NRSV)
1 Corinthians 15:51-58
Luke 6:39-49

The Transfiguration of Our Lord (Last Sunday after the Epiphany)
Exodus 34:29-35
Psalm 99
2 Corinthians 3:12—4:2
Luke 9:28-36 [37-43]

Ash Wednesday
Joel 2:1-2, 12-17
Psalm 51:1-18
(51:1-17 NRSV)
2 Corinthians 5:20b—6:10
Matthew 6:1-6, 16-21

First Sunday in Lent
Deuteronomy 26:1-11
Psalm 91:1-2, 9-16
Romans 10:8b-13
Luke 4:1-13

Second Sunday in Lent
Genesis 15:1-12, 17-18
Psalm 27
Philippians 3:17—4:1
Luke 13:31-35

Third Sunday in Lent
Isaiah 55:1-9
Psalm 63:1-8
1 Corinthians 10:1-13
Luke 13:1-9

Fourth Sunday in Lent
Joshua 5:9-12
Psalm 32
2 Corinthians 5:16-21
Luke 15:1-3, 11b-32

Fifth Sunday in Lent
Isaiah 43:16-21
Psalm 126
Philippians 3:4b-14
John 12:1-8

Sunday of the Passion /
Palm Sunday: Liturgy of the
Passion
Isaiah 50:4-9a
Psalm 31:9-16
Philippians 2:5-11
Luke 22:14—23:56

Monday in Holy Week
Isaiah 42:1-9
Psalm 36:5-11
Hebrews 9:11-15
John 12:1-11

Tuesday in Holy Week
Isaiah 49:1-7
Psalm 71:1-14
1 Corinthians 1:18-31
John 12:20-36

Wednesday in Holy Week
Isaiah 50:4-9a
Psalm 70
Hebrews 12:1-3
John 13:21-32

Maundy Thursday
Exodus 12:1-4 [5-10] 11-14
Psalm 116:1, 10-17
(116:1-2, 12-19 NRSV)
1 Corinthians 11:23-26
John 13:1-17, 31b-35

Good Friday
Isaiah 52:13—53:12
Psalm 22
Hebrews 10:16-25
John 18:1—19:42

The Resurrection of Our
Lord: Vigil of Easter
Genesis 1:1-2:4a
Genesis 7:1-5, 11-18; 8:6-
18; 9:8-13
Genesis 22:1-18
Exodus 14:10-31; 15:20-21
Isaiah 55:1-11
Proverbs 8:1-8, 19-21;
9:4b-6
Ezekiel 36:24-28
Ezekiel 37:1-14
Zephaniah 3:14-20
Jonah 3:1-10
Deuteronomy 31:19-30
Daniel 3:1-29
Romans 6:3-11
Luke 24:1-12

The Resurrection of Our
Lord: Easter Day
Acts 10:34-43
Psalm 118:1-2, 14-24
1 Corinthians 15:19-26
John 20:1-18

The Resurrection of Our
Lord: Easter Evening
Isaiah 25:6-9
Psalm 114
1 Corinthians 5:6b-8
Luke 24:13-49

Second Sunday of Easter
Acts 5:27-32
Psalm 118:14-29
Revelation 1:4-8
John 20:19-31

Third Sunday of Easter
Acts 9:1-6 [7-20]
Psalm 30
Revelation 5:11-14
John 21:1-19

Fourth Sunday of Easter
Acts 9:36-43
Psalm 23
Revelation 7:9-17
John 10:22-30

Fifth Sunday of Easter
Acts 11:1-18
Psalm 148
Revelation 21:1-6
John 13:31-35

Sixth Sunday of Easter
Acts 16:9-15
Psalm 67
Revelation 21:10, 22—22:5
John 14:23-29

The Ascension of Our Lord
Acts 1:1-11
Psalm 47
Ephesians 1:15-23
Luke 24:44-53

Seventh Sunday of Easter
Acts 16:16-34
Psalm 97
Revelation 22:12-14, 16-17, 20-21
John 17:20-26

Vigil of Pentecost
Exodus 19:1-9
Psalm 33:12-22
Romans 8:14-17, 22-27
John 7:37-39

The Day of Pentecost
Acts 2:1-21
Psalm 104:25-35, 37
(24-34, 35b NRSV)
Romans 8:14-17
John 14:8-17 [25-27]

The Holy Trinity (First Sunday after Pentecost)
Proverbs 8:1-4, 22-31
Psalm 8
Romans 5:1-5
John 16:12-15

Proper 3
Isaiah 55:10-13
Psalm 92:1-4, 12-15
1 Corinthians 15:51-58
Luke 6:39-49

Proper 4
1 Kings 8:22-23, 41-43
Psalm 96:1-9
Galatians 1:1-12
Luke 7:1-10

Proper 5
1 Kings 17:17-24
Psalm 30
Galatians 1:11-24
Luke 7:11-17

Proper 6
2 Samuel 11:26—12:10, 13-15
Psalm 32
Galatians 2:15-21
Luke 7:36—8:3

Proper 7
Isaiah 65:1-9
Psalm 22:18-27
(19-28 NRSV)
Galatians 3:23-29
Luke 8:26-39

Proper 8
1 Kings 19:15-16, 19-21
Psalm 16
Galatians 5:1, 13-25
Luke 9:51-62

Proper 9
Isaiah 66:10-14
Psalm 66:1-8
(66:1-9 NRSV)
Galatians 6:[1-6] 7-16
Luke 10:1-11, 16-20

Proper 10
Deuteronomy 30:9-14
Psalm 25:1-9
(25:1-10 NRSV)
Colossians 1:1-14
Luke 10:25-37

Proper 11
Genesis 18:1-10a
Psalm 15
Colossians 1:15-28
Luke 10:38-42

Proper 12
Genesis 18:20-32
Psalm 138
Colossians 2:6-15 [16-19]
Luke 11:1-13

Proper 13
Ecclesiastes 1:2, 12-14;
2:18-23
Psalm 49:1-11
(49:1-12 NRSV)
Colossians 3:1-11
Luke 12:13-21

Proper 14
Genesis 15:1-6
Psalm 33:12-22
Hebrews 11:1-3, 8-16
Luke 12:32-40

Proper 15
Jeremiah 23:23-29
Psalm 82
Hebrews 11:29—12:2
Luke 12:49-56

Proper 16
Isaiah 58:9b-14
Psalm 103:1-8
Hebrews 12:18-29
Luke 13:10-17

Proper 17
Proverbs 25:6-7
Psalm 112
Hebrews 13:1-8, 15-16
Luke 14:1, 7-14

Proper 18
Deuteronomy 30:15-20
Psalm 1
Philemon 1-21
Luke 14:25-33

Proper 19
Exodus 32:7-14
Psalm 51:1-11
(51:1-10 NRSV)
1 Timothy 1:12-17
Luke 15:1-10

Proper 20
Amos 8:4-7
Psalm 113
1 Timothy 2:1-7
Luke 16:1-13

Proper 21
Amos 6:1a, 4-7
Psalm 146
1 Timothy 6:6-19
Luke 16:19-31

Proper 22
Habakkuk 1:1-4; 2:1-4
Psalm 37:1-10
(37:1-9 NRSV)
2 Timothy 1:1-14
Luke 17:5-10

Proper 23
2 Kings 5:1-3, 7-15c
Psalm 111
2 Timothy 2:8-15
Luke 17:11-19

Proper 24
Genesis 32:22-31
Psalm 121
2 Timothy 3:14—4:5
Luke 18:1-8

Proper 25
Jeremiah 14:7-10, 19-22
Psalm 84:1-6 (84:1-7 NRSV)
2 Timothy 4:6-8, 16-18
Luke 18:9-14

Proper 26
Isaiah 1:10-18
Psalm 32:1-8
2 Thessalonians 1:1-4, 11-12
Luke 19:1-10

Proper 27
Job 19:23-27a
Psalm 17:1-9
2 Thessalonians 2:1-5, 13-17
Luke 20:27-38

Proper 28
Malachi 4:1-2a
Psalm 98
2 Thessalonians 3:6-13
Luke 21:5-19

Christ the King
Jeremiah 23:1-6
Psalm 46
Colossians 1:11-20
Luke 23:33-43

Reformation Day
Jeremiah 31:31-34
Psalm 46
Romans 3:19-28
John 8:31-36

All Saints' Day
Daniel 7:1-3, 15-18
Psalm 149
Ephesians 1:11-23
Luke 6:20-31

Day of Thanksgiving
Deuteronomy 26:1-11
Psalm 100
Philippians 4:4-9
John 6:25-35